# HOW TO KICK-ASS:

## Tools for combat

## TERRY BIRCH

Copyright © 2023 Terry Birch

ISBN: 978-1-923078-01-7
Published by Vivid Publishing
A division of Fontaine Publishing Group
P.O. Box 948, Fremantle
Western Australia 6959
www.vividpublishing.com.au

A catalogue record for this
book is available from the
National Library of Australia

# CAUTION

It is essential that before attempting any of the physical activities described or depicted in this book, the reader or readers should consult a qualified physician to ascertain whether the reader or readers should engage in the physical activity described or depicted in this book.

The physical activities  described herein may be overly taxing or sophisticated for the reader or readers, it is essential that this advice be followed and a physician consulted.

# INTRODUCTION

This is not a book that shows some techniques, kata or a style but how to fight. Real defence and application to look after yourself when needs be. This book was not intended to accumulate a thousand techniques but to show the best basic movements and rules about learning principles, footwork, timing to body mechanics and learning angles, directness in striking and kicks. True fighting efficiency, efficiency in body movement. If anyone practicing a martial art or any form of self/ defence, look for the truth in it. You can improve and give yourself more insight into what your practicing , maybe see what techniques are failing in your art or other martial art styles. Movements which are just movements that do not help to defend yourself after all.

1:   There are silly wasted movements. Impractical

2:   Punches which are easily telegraphed or

3:   In realistic circumstances blocks that will not block a punch or kick due to petty unrealistic techniques.

This book was originally done to give people something to learn self/defence to protect themselves in a world which some people are out of control but in the end it is a book about fighting for anyone who wants to learn and appreciate martial arts from beginners to the advanced.

The fundamentals and principles are for the advanced or for the beginner ready to go on a journey into fighting arts.

Part 3[upper body] and Part4 [lower body] which are shown are direct and simple but effective strikes. There are hundreds of movements, techniques if researched yourself but I have chosen but a few which are the most simple but are devastating and true to fighting situations. If your dedicated and in reasonable shape you can have the basics set in six months.

Love body movement is the key. Keep stretching to make movements easier and faster. Do some weight workouts. Run, ride and kick that bag. Train hard. It depends on how much time you put in to your training to how much better at self/defence you will be, but nothing is more important than the movements, mechanics and principles. Keep at it with the physical and mental, perfecting the movements. The spiritual will come. I hope this book may lead you on a journey of some sort. May it be a physical, mental or a journey of self discovery. Not just for self/defence but also giving you confidence, good communication skills like being kind to others or being compassionate to the Unfortunate. This would make everything most worth it!

When practiced with commitment and passion the martial arts will become effortless and the true art form of body movement will appear to you in your heart. This is true art. The benefits are endless.

# CONTENTS

# FUNDAMENTALS
# AND
# PRINCIPLES

# SPEED AND TIMING

Speed is an important aspect to martial art fighting. Without speed also timing you will have a tough time hitting your opponent. Increased speed gives you more power with each strike, also training for speed will allow you to move faster than your opponent. So you will be quicker to the punch, also it enables you to manifest more attacks in same specified amount of time. Speed is Important for both offence and defence. Simply speed gives advantage in getting to locking opponent to takedowns and striking first.etc. Also in defence helping you escape certain strikes by sliding to evading with feet to parrying,blocking. Speed in reacting [ Reaction time] contributes to speed. Timing, speed, distance are a trio, There is not one without the other. Practice techniques, striking, takedowns or whatever over and over again. Get your mind/body to strike, move when an opening presents itself. This is called motor learning. The time it takes between your mind then body to react. Your brain sends messages [like lightning bolts] to your body to react then you strike. A man who is disciplined in kungfu or boxing to a man who does not, the difference in reaction time is only a fraction of a second. So practicing techniques in sparring is a must. To achieve a great level of speed is difficult. You must workout your body so as to have:

1: Low level of body fat, so no extra Weight to slow you down.

2: High density muscle is a good Ingredient for high achievement in speed.

3: Having tension in your muscles slows you down, warm up, get blood moving, have a stretch routine, A flexible body gives you speed. Stretching before and after a workout is a must for training for speed.

Basically speed and good timing, having the right distance are as one. Speed in footwork allows you to break in/out of distance.

# DISTANCE

Distance is the measurement between you and your opponent which is continually shifting. A good fighter stays just out of reach of his opponent but not to far away so you can't strike. Moving in/out of opponents reach is a skill that takes a lot of practice.

1:  Good light footwork,

2:  using right distance,

3:  broken up Rhythm,

4:  good evasive skills, right timing.

Each fighter should be trying to break ground to strike, to Obtain the distance in which suits him by having a great sense of timing and by having a strategy of some sort for breaking distance for a strike. Like drawing your opponent forward within distance by leaving an opening for him. It will bring him forward in striking distance. You can counter his move knowing what he is going to do. Where he is going to strike. Or surprise him by feinting, looking like you're going to attack High, sticking a hand out towards his face but with no intention in it only to surprise him by sliding in, hitting him low. In the end a good fighter has good footwork, breaks distance, has good judgement in timing, knows right distance between him and his opponent.

# STRIKING DISTANCES

A diagram of the four types of distances in fighting.

1*: The distance in close fighting in which you can clinch, grabbing, strike with knees and elbows, arm bars, sweeps to biting and pinching.

2*: Punching distance.

3*: Kicking distance.

4*: Breaking distance in which you're making ground in a step And slide or push and slide. Also the run and jump kick. etc, all before a kick.

4a*: One can also break distance with a step and slide or push and slide to punch.

Practice in all distances, kicking and punching, clinching and grabbing, using knees and elbows in different ways. Moving in/out of distances is good practice. Good footwork is needed in keeping the right distance for either offence or defence.

# STANCE:

# THE FIGHTING READY POSITION [Good form]

The most important aspect of good form is to keep everything simple, while there are still a few rules involved. Good form is about body positioning in fighting and keeping a good natural stance, also simple footwork in sparring.

All kicks and punches are done from starting ready position.

After a strike is performed your arm or leg is returned back to The beginning, fighting ready position. Done in a fast rapid pace. So [ready position, bang/ hit, return to ready position.

Front hand position - Your front hand in a natural fighting Position should be high in front of you but not to high so it Obstructs the view of your opponent. Placed just under your eye line for a feeler, to feint or to strike out hard.

Also for defence in if you need to parry.

The hand approximately 12inches in front of you. Not to far forward that you don't generate any power. Practice and Adjust for what's natural to you. What feels good for you?

Rear hand position. – Your rear hand is just in front of your chin, or can be just touching the chin to protect the face.

Don't drop your hand to far down, practice keeping it up!

Your hand only moves away to parry or punch or whatever but remember your hands must come back fast.

Your elbow should be covering your kidneys and forearm covering your ribs. The rear hand is there to protect from straight punches and also wide swinging kicks and punches like the round house kick or the left and right hook.

So with your rear arm:

1:   The fist protects the face.

2:   The elbow protects the kidneys.

3:   The forearm protects the ribs.

# PRINCIPLES: GOOD FORM

The next aspect is be relaxed when sparring or fighting, not stiff, knees slightly bent, you know, feel balanced relaxed and alert.

When fighting or sparring you always move around on the balls of your feet. Not jumping around but moving, watching ready to spring and attack with the hands and feet straight towards the target.

Now in the circumstances fighting is continually shifting, moving left or right ducking and weaving so keeping the ready stance with feet and hands can be tough. Fighting will never go to plan.

Never have a plan. Remember keep everything simple.

When opponent punches you move or parry. You see an opening then you strike. After a few years you will not think, your body will just react or respond to the situation.

Your body will defend when need too or attack. Whatever is unfolding in front of you.

If you duck low for any reason and your hands are down but you see an opening hit from where your fists are. Straight from where they are too straight to your target.

1: If you see an opening, punch from where your hands are. Don't waste an opportunity.

2: Get back to ready position immediately.

Try using straight punches starting from…

1: Ready position. [Fighting position]

2: Then from any position your hands are at, at that time you're ready to punch. Duck or side/step then hit, bang.

Basically don't bring your fist back to your hip or move them too far away from the fighting position unnecessarily. The reasons why you must keep your fists up:

1: No wasted motion, you will be ready to counter/ strike. Defend or attack.

2: It will be very hard for them to telegraph what's coming at them.

3: Easier to hit your target. Your fists are there.

4: You won't lose your invitation to hit him. The opening won't be missed. There is less chance your opponent will bob or move away at the time you see an opening to strike.

Kicking has the same principle as punching, you kick straight to the target with no wasted motion. Meaning none of this jumping kicks or spinning kicks. This is done in the movies but not in real fighting. Your objective is to knock your attacker down and walk away!

Spinning kicks are great to practice for balance, agility and variety in training. Its fun but not recommended in Real fighting.

I recommend front foot kicks cause, well its faster. Its faster cause the front foot is closer to the target. But also you must change things up or an experienced fighter will know what coming. Surprise him by using your back foot.

Back foot kicks are slower but more powerful. Reason is the kick has more travelling time in which it gains more momentum till the kick hits the target. But it's easier to see It coming though, so easier to move out of distance.

When using front kicks you must practice putting a snap into your kicks. Like a whip into your kick to create power.

To make punching and kicking a fast, powerful and a beautiful flowing movement you need to use good footwork.

# FOOTWORK

Footwork is the main ingredient to me as to being a great Martial artist. Good footwork with balance, timing with the right distance all combined makes a great fighter.

First of all learn the basics.

1:  Your feet should be a nice comfortable distance apart to have good balance and quickness in manoeuvring around.

2:  Practice footwork in offence, striking moving forward Then defence, retreating backwards. Practice moving forwards to backwards, backwards then forwards.

Which means changing from left stance to right stance?

And vice versa.

3:  Practice moving in different directions going forwards to side stepping to retreating then going around circling your opponent moving clockwise to anticlockwise. While you're doing this remember your staying just out of distance of your opponent.

4:  Practice moving with a front foot slide to hit. Next back foot slide to hit. Next the step/slide to kick.

5:  Practice learning to defend against multiple attackers. It comes back to the basics. Pivoting and using your hips.

Remember your first day at karate. For me it was pivoting
And using the hips for power and changing direction!

Good memories, great sensei.

Here are some diagrams of footwork. Remember they
can be in reverse. [Either foot forward.]

You will see in the diagram why you need to be able to
Fight with either foot forward.

Diagram-

1:   Basic forward and backwards.

2:   Shuffle or slide to break distance.

    (a) Forward

    (b) Backwards

3:   Forward step/slide.

4:   Back foot slide to strike.

5:   Front foot step to hit at 180 degrees.

6:   Back foot step to hit at 180 degrees.

7:   Pivot and hit at 180 degrees.

8    (a) Direction change to the right.

    (b) Direction change to the left.

9:   Circling right and circling left.

10:  Stepping left, stepping right.

# (1) Basic Forwards to Backwards / Vice versa

**TOP VIEW**

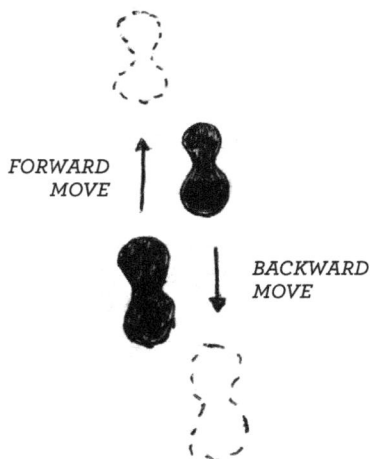

FORWARD MOVE

BACKWARD MOVE

# (2) Shuffle or slide. [To break distance]

**FORWARD/ATTACK**

*[3parts]*

*(1) This one is a push of the front foot first.*

*(2) Then back foot comes [shuffles] forward.*

*(3) The front foot slides forward.*

**MOVING BACKWARDS. [RETREATING]**

*[3parts]*

*(1) Push of the back foot.*

*(2) Front foot slides back, with the motion going backwards.*

*(3) Back foot shuffles back.*

# (3) Forward Step/slide: [to strike]

This is a hand strike or a front foot kick.

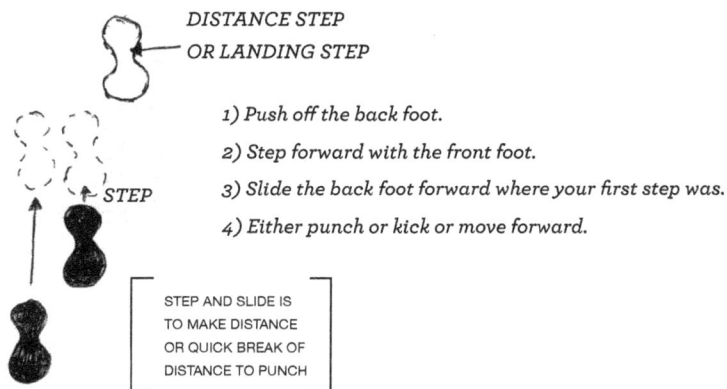

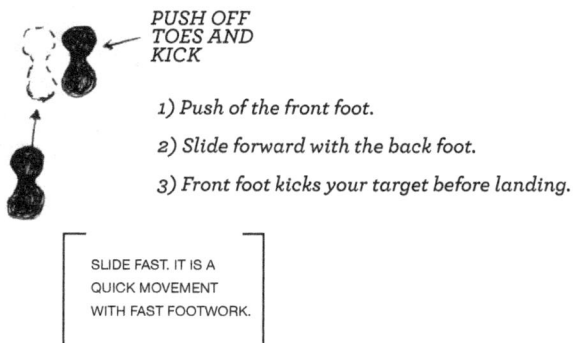

*DISTANCE STEP*
*OR LANDING STEP*

*STEP*

*1) Push off the back foot.*

*2) Step forward with the front foot.*

*3) Slide the back foot forward where your first step was.*

*4) Either punch or kick or move forward.*

STEP AND SLIDE IS
TO MAKE DISTANCE
OR QUICK BREAK OF
DISTANCE TO PUNCH

# (4) Back foot Slide to kick:

(Front foot kick)

*PUSH OFF*
*TOES AND*
*KICK*

*1) Push of the front foot.*

*2) Slide forward with the back foot.*

*3) Front foot kicks your target before landing.*

SLIDE FAST. IT IS A
QUICK MOVEMENT
WITH FAST FOOTWORK.

# (5) Front foot step/ hit @ 180 Degrees.

## Front foot step.

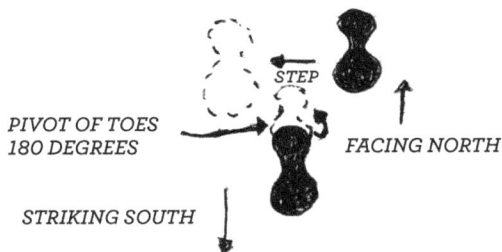

PIVOT OF TOES
180 DEGREES

STRIKING SOUTH

STEP

FACING NORTH

1) Step left if the right foot is forward. [Or vice versa]

2) Pivot off the back foot to become your front foot, pivot 180 degrees.

Stay on the toes with the pivot until the end of the movement. Swap your stance so you learn how to change directions.

---

# (6) Back foot step/hit @ 180 Degrees.

## Back foot step.

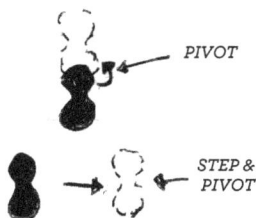

PIVOT

STEP & PIVOT

1) First step to your right with the back foot.

2) Next pivot with the front foot to make it the back foot. It's a pivot at 180 degrees so you strike an attacker from behind. Can be a punch forward to a punch behind.

# (7) Pivot and hit: 180 degrees

*A quick way to turn.*

**Backwards**                    **Forwards**

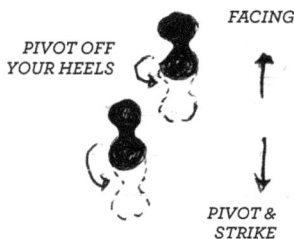

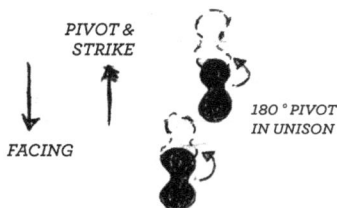

It's an easy move in which you pivot on your heals at 180 degrees. Pivot in unison. Practice pivoting on the Heals going backwards to forwards over and over again. It's quite a fun exercise, just remember to keep your balance.

# (8) Direction change at 90 degrees

\* Remember to change your stance with this one.\*

**To left**                              **To right**

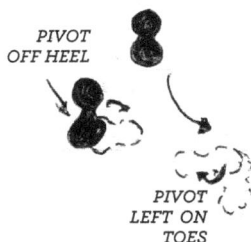

With the direction change stepping right, with the back foot you pivot on the heal not the toes or your feet will be too far apart. You will be off balance or your opponent can easily push you of balance.

# (9) Basic circling:

## Circling right

Basically if your front foot is the right foot you circle right.

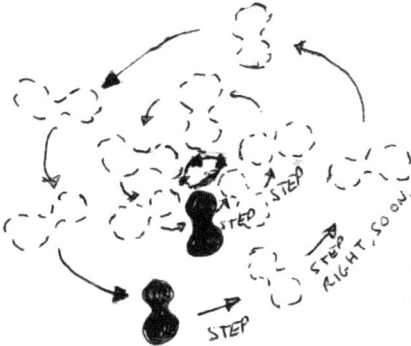

*1) STEP WITH YOUR FRONT FOOT FIRST.*
*2) STEP WITH THE BACK FOOT NEXT.*

## Circling left

Same as above but you circle left as your front foot is your left foot.

REMEMBER TO KEEP YOUR OPPONENT OR ATTACKER IN FRONT OF YOU AT ALL TIMES!!

# (10) Stepping left/ stepping right:

*LEFT TO RIGHT.*

1) *Push of the back foot.*

2) *Step with the front foot.*

3) *Then back foot.*

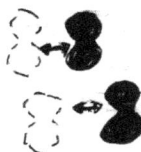

*RIGHT TO LEFT.*

1) *Push of the front foot.*

2) *Step with the back foot.*

3) *Then front foot.*

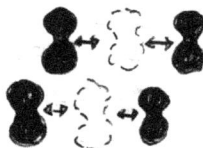

It's a small step but just enough to parry or evade a strike. Stepping left or right, circling left or right is found in boxing. A good boxer uses both feet.

Being able to strike with all limbs in whatever stance is essential. Only being able to fight with one foot forward is limited. This may be done in sport but not in real fighting!

Simply you want to be able to move in any direction and strike with all limbs.

Good footwork gives you speed in movement from start to finish which is from the first move of the feet to the end of the strike. A kick or punch or whatever strike. To add power, footwork with the use of the hips is essential for power hitting with either the legs or arms. Also shifting your weight from back foot through to your front foot in unison creates power. Remember power comes from the legs first.

## FOOTWORK: DEFENCE STRATEGY

TO RESTART OR RESET: With an attacker who's strategy is to come at you quick and hard with kicks and punches to keep you on the defence till they knock you down can be overwhelming.

The human instinct is to back up and back up until eventually he knocks you down. To over come this a good technique is to step left or right depending on which foot is forward will momentarily stop his striking so you can restart. (I call it the hallway step or elevator step. No circling in here man.)

# Deadly Techniques
# + Target Areas

# Deadly techniques:

This section is for people who are attacked and think there life is threatened in anyway.

These techniques are used to escape an attacker so you can get some help either from a passing person or your Local police officer.

In war-time deadly unarmed techniques are used to kill. There are many deadly movements but again I am going to show simple movements also common sense without going too far into the martial arts. Remember we are escaping an attacker to get help.

Deadly movements are usually aimed at the eyes, throat, groin and knees to immobilize the enemy.

Deadly strikes can be done by either sex. Young or old. You don't need to be strong but fast, quick to get the job done and escape your attacker.

Some techniques are:

**Biting** is a very effective in close combat. It is mainly used when your restraint, there is no other possible way out of the situation. The jaw is the strongest muscle in the body.

**Hair pulling** is a good way to escape an attacker. If they have hair?

**The Finger Jab** is traditionally a leading hand or front hand strike to the eyes. But I think it can be whatever hand as  long as it works, escaping your attacker. Just strike out as quick as you can with your fingers. Not much power is needed to jab out your attackers eyes.

This is a technique only used in the worst circumstances.

**The Throat** is another area of the body which will drop Or maim your attacker to get away. Strike out with any hit to the throat. The most common strike is the popular traditional open hand karate chop. The palm facing up or your palm facing down. Striking from the front or side of your attacker.

**The Head Butt** is a devastating close combat move. It is better used when using the side or back of the head. Used when you are in a bear hug or when the attacker is close holding you from behind. Just thrust back your head hoping To hit him on the nose. In kung fu they stomp hard on the foot to hurt and surprise him then immediately thrust back with the head. I don't recommend head butting with your forehead as it will hurt and may knock YOU out!

**The Groin** is a good target spot to hit to get away from an attacker. The groin can be struck from the front, side or behind. You don't need a lot of power to drop a big attacker, You mainly need accuracy. Any simple kick can hit your target. Obviously grabbing his groin with your hands will make him cry! If your attacker is behind you, lift your leg up and hit the groin with the heal of the foot. This is the best way to drop him to escape the situation. If being held, your attacker is grabbing you from the front simply knee them in the groin. This is simple but effective. All of these movements or techniques if you will are very simple and can be done by anyone. Big or small, male or female. More shown on these techniques in Chapter 2. Upper body, also Chapter 3 Lower body.

# TARGET AREAS

While fighting, many people aim for the head area, but their are many areas of the body in which to strike?

When practicing your different strikes with your hands and feet always try hitting all parts of the body from the head to the feet. Break it up by hitting the nose, then maybe cracking a few ribs, to a lower side kick to the knees.

There are many different combinations and ways to practice hitting the target areas of the body and is only limited by You're Imagination.

Remember to use all your body parts to hit, in which I mean, use your fingers to strike the eyes, strike with your knees, elbows, head, hands or feet and strike at all the target areas.

Some off these areas are only to be striked at in life-threatening situations, striking any of these areas are dangerous and should be carried out for self/defence purposes only.

# TARGET AREAS:

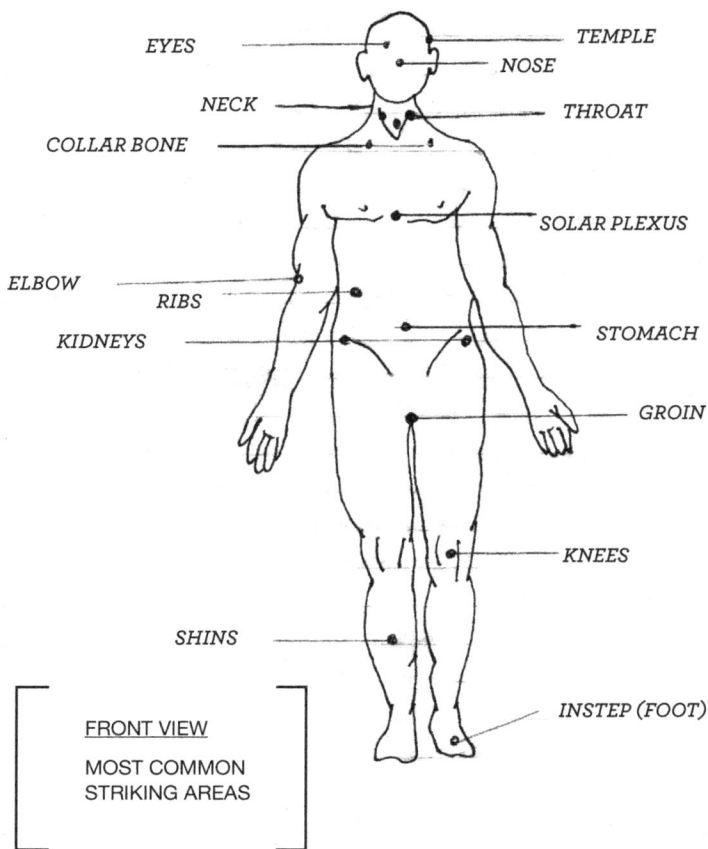

EYES — TEMPLE

NOSE

NECK — THROAT

COLLAR BONE

SOLAR PLEXUS

ELBOW

RIBS

KIDNEYS — STOMACH

GROIN

KNEES

SHINS

INSTEP (FOOT)

FRONT VIEW

MOST COMMON
STRIKING AREAS

Striking areas from a back view is anywhere along the spine from just under the skull to the lower back.

# BLOCKING AND PARRYING

A parry is basically a deflection of any strike thrown at you. You need a quick smooth movement with good timing to execute a parry. The two outside parry areas are the ones in which the front foot and arm are forward. The two inside parry areas are from the rear hand. The four parry areas protect the area from the forehead to the knees.

All the four parry areas are done by a rotation of the elbows, deflecting a strike with the forearm or hand. After a short time practicing these parry's they will come natural to you, there will be no high or low, outside or Inside parry, just a deflection of the strike. The hard part is the timing. Sparring or fighting is the only way to have excellence in parry's. Skill in timing is what makes a fighter.

# The Four Basic Parrying Areas:

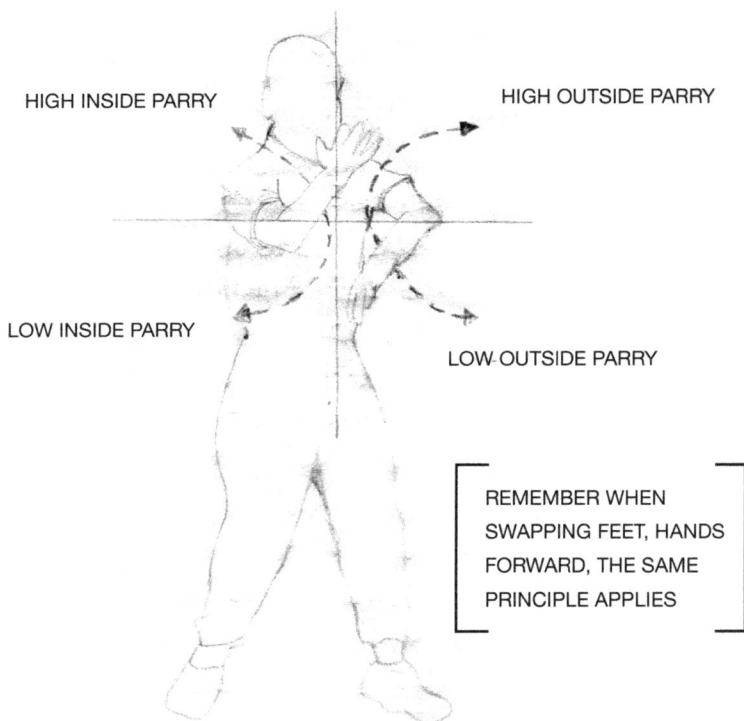

HIGH INSIDE PARRY

HIGH OUTSIDE PARRY

LOW INSIDE PARRY

LOW OUTSIDE PARRY

REMEMBER WHEN
SWAPPING FEET, HANDS
FORWARD, THE SAME
PRINCIPLE APPLIES

All of these parry's go from the inside out, which is the  from the body deflecting away. Remember when practicing these parry's, to protect a greater area you must lift your elbow slightly to protect your nose or lower your elbow to protect your groin, but don't change the elbow rotation.

When you parry just do enough to deflect the strike from Its path. That is all is needed. If you deflect the strike and move your arm to far away from the body you will be vulnerable to another strike in the same area. Another word make sure you have control in your movement. If you're against a fighter who is taller with longer reach it is better to parry while taking a step backwards, the actual parry takes place as you step, not afterward. With a taller opponent I would bob, weave or duck than parry.

Evading: By slipping or weaving it can leave wide openings for you to counter attack. In defence you can practice dodging the strike at you by weaving or bobbing to side stepping or taking a step backwards out of reach. Blocking: The only block.

# The Lower Block

Here is a basic lower block which is easy to do. You must practice this many times even if it looks simple to make it a natural movement. It is just a drop of the hand to protect the groin area. It can be made by either hand. This block is used if your to slow to step back or in the middle of stepping back.

## More on blocking

A parry is much better to use than blocking. When blocking your stopping and absorbing a great amount of force which can hurt compared to deflecting the force away.

In blocking having the full force hit your arm or leg can knock you off balance, creating openings for the attacker to take advantage.

But in the lower block situation a block is better than a kick to the groin!

With the lower block and the variations of the semi circular parry's a defence- counter to attack can be used. This is a parry and punch used at the same time. This can be done by a step forward with a parry and punch or seeing your opponent step forward while you hold your ground then parry and punch together. This is a defence movement turned into an attack. This technique or movements is all about timing. More on defence counter to attack shown in the upper-body section.

## The high parry

The high parry is a parry with the hand coming across your face. Either with a slip or without a slip.

A slip is a slight movement of your body to move out of normally a lead jab. The slipping movement is so small it Doesn't change your initial attack or movement forward. Make sure when you parry your opponent strikes, you are well-balanced and that you parry the punch just enough to miss your head.

After you parry, your opponent will spin of balance and will leave him self open to be hit, either to the head or ribs

# (The counter attack)

You can either parry and punch at the same-time or parry Then punch. A high parry can be done with either the rear hand or lead hand. It depends on what angle the strike comes at you to which hand deflects the strike?

Again this is another movement which needs great awareness and timing to pull-off in real fighting. This movement needs practice to make it a natural movement.

# STRETCHING

The following is a basic Introduction to a warm up and stretch routine.

There is a stretch routine so your body will be ready to deliver fast and strong kicks and punches.

Stretching is most important and just one aspect to being a good martial artist. One thing also is to enjoy stretching and make it a part of your training. Make it serious but also make it fun!

## Stretching - (Warm-up)

First, warming up before stretching is crucial, warming up the body produces an increase in muscle . The flexibility of joints and muscles is more easily achieved after a proper warm up period, increasing the range of motion and elasticity of a muscle. By doing a few warm up exercises your body will be prepared for demanding stretching exercises, you will be able to exert more pressure on the muscles, joints and tendons without causing an injury.

Here are a few warm up exercises:

1) Treadmill or, run on spot.-3x1 min Intervals. I jog around the oval doing 3 laps, walk 1, with a 1km jog to finish.

2) Exercise bike is great for a warm up. But don't over do it!

3) Stepping on a chair - alternating legs. My step ups are performed on a crate with little rest periods.

4) Sets of push ups

5) Star jumps

6) Sets of sit-ups

7) Skip with your skipping rope.

Choose your exercises to warm up and make it fun!

## Stretching - (Flexibility)

Flexibility refers to the possible range of motion or movement of a joint or a group of joints.

Stretching improves the range of movement of a muscle. If you stretch daily or regularly, your muscles capacity to extend fully is increased allowing the joint a greater range of movement. The increased range of movement will give you greater speed and power to your kicks and punches.

With regular stretching, muscles will be loose, supple, so that when called upon to perform a kick or fast punch you will be able to extend to the full range of movement without resulting in an injury, damaging the muscle tissue.

Again, limited flexibility results in restricted movement or injury. Resulting in loss of practice.

## The following are basic principles involving Stretching:

- Stretch only when the muscles are warmed up.

- Breathe slowly and evenly.

- Do not over stretch. Go to the point where the stretch is felt but no pain. (If you over stretch the opposite result can happen. Reduction in muscle flexibility.)

- Hold the stretch for 15-30 seconds or longer if possible.

- No bouncy or jerky movements. Slowly go to the stretched position.

- Stretch before and after a sparring or martial arts session.

Before stretching or any training always start with some gentle warm-ups for the joints and ligaments.

Which are:  - Wrists          - Knees

               - Elbows          - Shoulders. (Deltoids)

               - Hips              - Lower back.

# A Warm up: (Light stretch)

WRIST CIRCLES: With your arms out, rotate the wrists around in circles one way 10 times, then the other way 10 times.

ELBOW CIRCLES: With the arms out in front rotate the elbows in circles one way 10 times, then the other way 10 times.

*TIP: Like the wrist exercise, when rotating your elbows, One elbow will go in a clockwise direction while the other in an anticlockwise direction.*

ARM CIRCLES: To loosen the shoulders stretch your arms straight up above the head and begin moving your arms forward and down, going in big circles.

10 times going forwards, 10 times backwards.

*TIP: Don't swing the arms to fast, just a nice smooth pace.*

KNEE CIRCLING: Stand with your feet shoulder width apart with your hands on the knees. Begin rotating your knees in one direction 10 times, then the other direction 10 times.

HIP CIRCLING: Stand with your feet shoulder width

apart with your hands on your hips. Begin moving your torso in a clock wise direction 10times then anticlock-wise 10 times.

HIP AND BACK CIRCLING: Raise your hands above your  head, and then begin rotating your waist and hips to the right, then down touching the floor (if you can) with fingers, continue rotating waist in an arc until you return to the starting position. (hands above the head.) Do it 10 times in one direction then 10 times in the other direction.

*TIPS:*

*1) Beginners begin with the feet a little more than shoulder width.*

*2) Keep your knees locked through out the exercise.*

*3) Arms stretched out through out the exercise.*

*4) Stay tight to your body and rotate in a big arc while keeping a nice even pace.*

Here are some of the main stretches for flexibility:

Remember for beginners only go to point of stretch which is comfortable for you. Do not overstretch.

## QUADRICEP STRETCH:

Stand and bring one heel back up to your buttocks. Hold your ankle, make sure the other leg is straight. Keep your knees together. Hold, relax. Then change legs, repeat.

## STANDING CALF STRETCH: (Wall)

Face a wall and place both hands against the wall at shoulder height. Have both feet backwards until your right leg, torso and arms make a straight line. The left leg should be bent. Press your heel down to the floor. Hold, relax and change legs. Repeat.

---

*TIP: If it's too comfortable, to intensify the stretch put your foot back a couple of inches.*

---

# LOWER BACK STRETCH/ HAMSTRINGS:

1)  Stand erect with your hands on your lower back.

2)  Keep your hands on your lower back and lean backwards as far as possible. Hold for a 10 seconds.

3)  Then lean forwards and down as far as possible. As you start to lean forwards bring your hands over head, as you bend down, try to touch your hands to your toes. Hold for 10 seconds. Repeat. Do 5 repetitions.

## HAMSTRING VARIATIONS:
## Touching toes:

Lean forward while keeping your back straight, try touching your toes like the previous stretching exercise. Now grab your left angle. Pull your head to your left knee. Hold. Now grab your right ankle. Pull your head to your right knee. Hold. Next move towards the centre. Hold.    Stand up, relax, and repeat 5 times.

*TIPS: Do not over stretch past the point of tension. Do this exercise slowly with no bouncy movements.*

## LUNGE STRETCH:

Stand erect with your hand on the hips. Step forward with either leg and bend fully with the front leg while keeping the back leg straight. Stretch. Hold. Relax then change legs. Repeat 3 times with each leg. The front thighs, hip and buttocks get a stretch.

## SEATED GROIN STRETCH:

Start by placing the heels together and resting the elbows on the knees, your heels also should be against your pelvis. Now with your elbows exert pressure on the knees pushing them to the floor. Hold for 15 seconds, relax, and repeat 5 times.

## SEATED HAMSTRING STRETCH:

Sit on the floor and extend one leg forward, straight out locking the knee throughout the movement. The other leg should be bent with the heel resting against the inner thigh of the extended leg. Now with the back straight reach out towards your ankle and down so your chin touches your knee. Hold 15 seconds. Change legs, repeat 3-5 times.

## LOWER BACK, INNER THIGH SEATED STRETCH

Sit with your legs spread as far apart as possible, lean forward and reach out with your chest down to the floor, plus have your arms reached out forward as well. Hold, relax. Now turn your body and reach out to your right ankle, reaching out with your hands and chest forward and down. Hold. Now turn to your left ankle, repeat by doing the same action as the previous two.

*TIP: Keep your back straight throughout the exercise.*

# HAMSTRING STRETCH: (USING A BAR)

Place one leg on a bar. Legs straight with the knees locked. With the foot that's on the bar point the toes towards you to get the maximum stretch. Place your hands on your knee and gently reach forward with your head while your stomach is down towards the thigh. Hold for 15 seconds or more, go back to starting position. Relax. Repeat 5 times. Change legs and repeat exercise.

# 2 LEG RAISE STRETCHING EXERCISES:

These two leg raise exercises are done when your muscles have been stretched and warmed up.

HAMSTRING EXERCISE:

Start at the ready position. Now swing your back leg forward up in an arc trying to bring the leg up as far as you can, bringing the knee close to your chest at the top end of the movement. The toes should be trying to point towards you. Then lower back to start ready position.

*TIP: The support foot heel should be grounded throughout the entire movement. Change legs, repeat 2 sets of ten.*

## GROIN STRETCH EXERCISE:

Starting position- Stand upright with the feet together touching at the ankles and toes pointing forward. Hands on thighs. With one leg bring it out then up in an arc to the side of you keeping the toes pointing forward. Bring your leg up as far as you can keeping the body in an upright position, then lower it back, follows the same arc. Repeat ten times. Change legs. Ten more. You should feel a nice stretch in the groin area.

*TIP: Keeping good balance is needed in the two leg raising exercises. For beginners hold on to a chair or wall is recommended for support so you get a nice flowing movement to get maximum stretch.*

# Upper Body

# UPPER BODY STRIKES: (INTRO)

While practicing these hand strikes use these movements in the correct form. (Way)

In the pictures watch how I always have my rear hand ready for a parry or strike. This is good practice, having it in a nice position no matter what. Be ready to strike or counter strike.

Always think to attack. Your rear hand should be open for a parry, loose and ready but when it comes out to sting, it shuts before it connects! You must do the movements in a flowing manner. Practice these punches till you have good body feel doing it at ease and good flow. Till it's a natural movement to you. As a beginner it may take Sometime to get the right body feel.

Once you have the right technique add speed to your punches while keeping your balance and right body positioning. By adding speed to your punches you will add more power. While practicing your hand strikes use the right mental attitude in which I mean, smash that punching bag. Concentrate and have nothing else on your mind. At home there are a lot of distractions so you need to focus and have attitude to each punch. So you must have-

1) Quickness but good form, good form then develop devastating speed.

2) Direction- Make sure every punch is going to hit where it is suppose too.

3) Generate your power from good body mechanics, by twisting and whipping the hips while rolling and pushing the shoulders out and also pivoting hard. All done together simultaneously. You can even get more power in your strikes by doing strength exercises using free weights like dumbbells, barbells etc.

So strength/ speed/ right technique = power.

To get more power, - Go to the gym. To get the most out of your hand strikes use a punching bag. Just punching a bag can be a great workout. A great cardio workout and endurance plus all out power.

Remember you will slowly but surely improve over time. Also obviously the more you practice the quicker and better your hand strikes will be. So practice, practice, practice!

# THE BACK FIST

Good footwork is needed to execute a powerful back fist. Like a spring, push of the back foot, roll your front foot from heel to toe and with momentum strike out a back fist. The back foot may lift of the ground a little bit. At the end of the strike flick it hard at the wrists then bring it back. All done at the same speed from start to finish, in the correct flow. Keep your fist just slightly open till impact. The strike will be faster. Your hand will be relaxed being slightly open than closed. If you clench your fist tight you'll be stiff and slow, it won't have that snap at the end.

You can use the back fist any where in the 360* around you by using the right footwork. So it is a punch to use if there is more than one attacker.

A back fist is a simple punch but must be done with focus, with the right technique to make it a powerful punch.

# THE HAMMER FIST

A hammer fist punch is an offence strike in which the power comes from the legs and waist. Used when an attacker comes to the side of you or behind you. The hammer fist punch has a big swinging action. Do not use the hammer fist if the attacker is in front of you. There are faster hand strikes, more direct strikes to the target than a swinging arm strike. Its effectiveness is striking to the sides and behind. It's a very effective punch when there is more than one attacker. The hammer fist is a great punch to practice in combinations.

Example: Imagine two attackers. A straight punch to the attacker in front of you. Another attacker comes at you from the side so strike out a hammer fist. Very simple but effective.

With the hammer fist there are many areas of the body you can target. The

- Head          - Ribs

- Solar plexus   - Kidneys

- Stomach        - Groin

With the hammer fist you don't need to move your feet from your natural ready stance to strike out a hammer fist. It's just a pivot of the feet, whip of the waist and strike it hard out towards your target. Before your about to punch practice bringing the striking arm back a bit towards the chest, then swing out the hammer fist punch. Practice the movement making it a smooth action. Eventually you will make it a powerful fast punch. It is a very simple body action but you need to practice to make it an instinctive movement.

# OPEN HAND STRIKES

The open hand strikes target the neck, throat and head areas. With the open hand chop to the throat it is used only in a life or death situation.

Open hand strikes are very simple to do. If your enemy isn't in front of you well then the right foot work is needed.

Look in the foot work section:

5) Front foot step @ 180 degrees

6) Back foot step @ 180 degrees

7) Pivot and hit to 180 degrees

8) Direction change.

With the open hand strikes the palm can be facing up or down depending on the direction your going or what hand your striking with.

Also strike from where your hands are at the time. There is no need to bring the arm back before you strike. Practice these techniques with the right foot forward, then change feet to left foot forward.

# STRAIGHT PUNCHES

The core (or centre) of punching is the straight punch. The technique is simple but very important and takes a lot of practice to get power into it!

The foot work is easy also. There is no need to change from the natural fighting ready stance. With getting the right technique there are a few factors involved.

- First is getting the right alignment of the fist (wrist) to along the forearm to the shoulder. On impact your arm should be in a straight line from the knuckles to your shoulder. Timing is needed. Practice.

- Your fist should also be vertical at all times. It is the most natural position to have the fist vertical, also it can take the most impact without hurting your wrist. You will be able to punch the punching bag with power, also for longer.

- Next is after you punch bring your fist back fast to protect your body or to be ready to strike again. The speed of the punch does not end when the punch hits the target. It must come back to your natural ready fighting position just as quick From start to finish.

- Like all of the punches, turn your hip, whip the waist to get your power.

- Remember strike with attitude. When you punch you hit that bag as hard as you can. Hit through your target to destroy!!

- The best attribute of the straight punch is the directness. Always punch from where the hands are in a straight line towards your targets. Reason being:

1) You may miss your opportunity to hit.

2) Less travelling distance. eg (faster)

3) Less chance of your opponent seeing or reacting to your punch that's coming their way.

With the straight punches it is an attacking movement. Punching or moving forward towards the opponent. Either by parrying, slipping, ducking, evading or whatever but attack, attack, attack!! No backward step. Hit all parts of the body. Punches can go in variable angles. High or low, left or right but the same thing applies. Punch from where the hands are at the time, in a straight line to your target while using the right technique. (way) .With practice you will be able to perform a half dozen straight punches in quick time.

Now we will talk about the parry and straight punch. This is important. When you need to parry you can either-Parry then punch or parry and punch simultaneously, at the same time which takes a lot of practice.  In sparring, practice parrying and straight punching together.

1) Waiting for your opponent to move forward in distance.

2) You stepping forward attacking him.

3) Or if opponent likes doing wide swinging punches. Doing  them too many times.

MULTIPLE HITS: Practice combination punches in the 1, 2 also triple punches or as many strikes as you want, usually until you get tired and lose control of your balance and focus. By that I mean your not using the right technique. Your being sloppy and missing the target. When you are practicing combination punching to multiple attackers coming at you in all direction, focus on balance, timing and applying the right technique. Together they are hard enough to do without thinking of the feet. That is the reason why the foot work is kept very simple. Things you need to keep in mind in using straight punching combinations are:

1) Keep your balance. (You can be punching up to 10 times.)

2) Use the right technique for maximum power.

3) Keep focus ( Hit your targets)

Again while you practice in combinations use your imagination. Punch left or right, high to low.

# THE HOOK PUNCH

With the hook punch it is a wide punch in which the path of the fist comes from the side of the opponent. Out of there vision around his guard hitting him on the jaw. It can be used as a lead punch or part of combination punching, combinations with the straight punches or the back fist.

The hook can be used in combinations together from high to low or low to high. Left to right or right to left. With momentum the hooks are a powerful combination. The hook to the head mainly is a long hook but it has slight variations to the line or path to the head.

You have the sharp hook which is like a long hook but the path is shorter, not so wide it's straighter to the target.

You have the upward hook which comes underneath the chin. Don't get confused with the uppercut. An upward hook is a lot wider and comes at a wider angle.

So you have a long hook, sharp hook and the upward hook. You also have a short hook. The short hook is a close distance hook or infighting hook in which you can strike the stomach, kidneys, ribs or jaw. It depends on the distance or relationship you are to your opponent. The hook punch is used also when your opponent drops his hands to low, giving you the opportunity to go over his guard punching him on the jaw.

To me, combining the straight punches which are direct to the target with a hook, a wide line to the target is a great way to surprise even the best adversary. As mentioned the hook catches  your opponent of guard by coming outside of there vision.

TECHNIQUE:

1) Shift of body weight.

2) Pivot

3) Turn of hips

4) Punch through your target

5) On contact fist at 45 degrees

 - My version of a right hook is right foot forward, left foot back.

It's my favourite hook.

1) Starting from the ready fighting position. First your body  weight has to be shifted to the right foot. To do that sway the  hips clockwise a little, while doing the same with the back  foot. Just pivot on the toes bringing the back heal clockwise. The reason for the shift of the body weight is to bring more  weight into the punch for power.

2) Now with your right fist, punch and bring all that body  weight towards your target by pivoting on the

front foot and back foot (toes) and turning your hips (waist) with a whip, simultaneously. All done in a split second!

3) Now the body is going left and slightly forward towards the target. To bring down a big man you must punch through your target. Don't stop at the face or body, hit through him continuing the path of punch.

4) Your fist should be at 45 degrees on impact. The same thing applies to the upward hook, sharp hook or long hook. The hook is a punch that has longer travelling distance to the target but man it has power. In boxing a hook plays a major role in knockouts. Well it is a knockout punch!! Also if your going to do a left hook with right foot forward the same thing applies, only change is it's a rear hook. Nothing changes.


**Conclusion on punching:**

You are using all possible lines to your target that is in front of you by using the straight punches, the back fist and the various angled hooks. Upward hook, short hook, long hook and sharp hook! Movements that are fast if the right technique is performed.

# ELBOWS

Elbows are used in close quarter fighting. When using elbows you use all of your body weight behind each strike for devastation.

Elbows can strike at any angle. Up, down, left or right, high or low. All elbows are done at slight variations depending on the situation. Striking to the front, side or behind.

The following are some elbow strikes.

UPWARD ELBOW- If you're in close distance of your attacker push up with the legs and use the upward elbow. Put all of your body weight behind it! You can also take a step forward and use the upward elbow as well. Target to aim for is under the chin or nose. This one is a devastating blow and can cause harm or death. Practice but only use when you really need too!

DOWNWARD ELBOW- This is a move when you have already hit your attacker in the stomach or solar plexus and bends over, finishing him of with a downward elbow to the middle of his back. Target to aim is his spine to finish him off. In a life or death situation you aim for back of the neck. (Base of the skull.)

BACKWARD ELBOW. (Midsection)- Used when an attacker comes up behind you. A good target to aim for is the solar plexus, stomach or ribs.

BACKWARD ELBOW. (Head)- In one motion turn your head, lift your elbow and in a twist of the waist and roll of the shoulders aim for the temple, nose or jaw. Remember to practice either (both) side. (s)

SLIDE IN HIGH FRONT ELBOW. - This is a quick slide in elbow to the head. As shown in foot work section slide in by, pushing of the back foot and sliding in first with front foot followed by the back foot. All done in a fast simultaneous motion. Lift the elbow up and cock it back a bit then a forward hard strike to the face. This is a committed strike so lean the body into it.

SIDE ON FRONT ELBOW. - With a step, move in and turn side on to your opponent, with a bend of the knees strike out an elbow. Either under the arm of opponent cracking the ribs or front on hitting his solar plexus, stomach or head. This elbow is mainly done after a strike has stopped or startled the attacker this makes it easier to step in distance, but not always. You can also parry or duck a punch then move in with the elbow. If you can with the parry, hold on to the arm and use it as leverage pulling him forward, getting a stronger hit in.

FORWARD SWINGING ELBOW. - This movement is a pivot of the feet and a big rotation (twist) of the waist, with a roll of the shoulder. All of this done in good flow. The greater the pivot and twist of the hips the more power you will have. Also put your body behind it! Practice going one way then the other. This elbow move will show you the (importance) value of a good pivot and hip rotation.

ELBOWS: COMBINATIONS. – Once you have practiced and learnt each of the elbows use your imagination to come up with combinations of elbow strikes of your own. Here is a fun exercise to practice. Strike out first with a back fist then by using the front elbow come in and elbow under opponents arm then turn your body the other way and use the backward elbow or step forward hitting the attacker from behind.

# Lower Body

HOW TO KICK ASS

# Kicking- (Introduction)

All kicks start at the fighting ready position. Remember to practice on both legs, also to use the front foot and back foot if a kick uses both.

The front foot is closer to the target which makes it more effective. Good balance is needed to execute a quick powerful kick. Try not to move your hands to far away from the fighting position while you're kicking. After the kick you may need to defend so you don't want your hands too far away from the body. With all kicks practice till it's a nice easy flowing action then get some power into it. To get power in your kicks, practice on a heavy bag. Also to get accuracy in your kicks get a friend and use focus mitts. Even if you have nothing air kicking is good. Just practice, practice, practice!

There are 5 ways to practice your kicking. With these you will use the front foot, back foot and in combinations.

1) Kicking and dropping your striking foot down. But practice being aware of the distance between you and your opponent, what their doing. By dropping your foot down you may be in striking distance. If the opponent parry's your vulnerable to an easy counter. Practice kicking with the front foot then back foot.

2) Kicking and bringing your foot back behind you to fighting ready position. After your kick bring your

foot back to fighting ready position just as fast as the initial strike.  Practice kicking with the front foot then back foot.

3) Practice kicking forward 2 or 3 times. Practice advancing forward kicking with back foot then front foot. Change it up. Come forward kicking first with back foot and next two with the front foot. Whatever. Use your imagination.

4) Kicking to all directions. High to low. Left to right. In front of you to an attacker coming from behind.

5) Practice your kicking by using the foot work in the foot work section. The front foot step and slide to pivoting left or right. Study all foot work in the foot work section. Study it!

In sparring or in a fighting situation kicking to much or kicking for the sake of kicking is useless and takes up to much energy. Kick only when an opening presents itself. Also in practice so much energy is used so only practice your kicking 4 to 5 times a week. Especially if you run daily or you're in the gym doing squats. Etc. Your legs will need rest so alternate your martial art training with weight training. It's better to practice your kicks for 30 minutes daily with focus, spirit and power than 1 hour a day with tired legs and petty technique. In real fighting kicking your attacker from the waist down is recommended. The time it takes for your foot to travel the distance to the head your opponent can easerly move leaving you vulnerable to a counter strike or is easerly defended. You must remember we are talking about street fighting with no rules. A man trying to rip your head off!

But if an opening does present itself at their head kick with the front foot. Again not always it depends on the situation and relationship you are with your attacker or opponent. The front foot kicks are direct, simple and harder to defend. By being more flexible makes your kicks faster also gives you more target areas to choose from. The following are simple effective devastating kicks for real fighting situations.

We will start with straight kicks to round kicks and finish with combination kicking.

# STRAIGHT KICKS

KIN GERI: This is a simple kick; you just simply strike your leg up into the groin area much like kicking an A.F.L ball. The foot goes directly to the target in a quick action then back again. The Kin Geri kick is devistatation and does not matter the age, anyone can use it to escape an attacker.

SIDE KICK: The sidekick is a very powerful kick, devastating if done in the right technique. You can use either the front foot or back foot. Now the front foot is a more practical kick to use in many aspects.

- First the front foot is closer to your target (attacker) so less distance to travel, which makes it a much quicker strike.

- Less telegraphed, harder for your opponent to evade or defend.

- By using the proper footwork you can get good distance out of it. If your opponent steps back from a kick you will surprise him by being virtually in his face with a second kick. In the footwork section use:

(1) Forward attack.

(2) Forward step "n" slide.

(3) Back foot slide to strike.

With the sidekick you can hit any part of the body, it will hurt!

But when practicing you focus on hitting the weaker parts of the body.

- Head          - Ribs

- Solar plexus  - Knees

- Stomach       - Groin

- Throat.

With lots of practice with the sidekick, focus and you can strike precisely where you want to hit easerly. Occasionally change it up. Use the back foot or your opponent may eventually learn to counter your moves. Out of all the kicks the side kick is the most powerful. It's a very direct kick with the body weight behind the strike, with a snap at the end is what makes it the most powerful kick of all. Good balance and foot work is needed to execute a powerful sidekick. When practicing, relax keep your body centred, no leaning forwards or backwards and glide into the kick. Flow at a nice pace until it becomes natural to you then quicken the action till it becomes a deadly strike. You can either hit with the bottom of your foot or turn your foot and hit with the knife edge side of the foot. (From the little toe to the heal.)

FRONT KICK: (Mae Geri) - The front kick is another fast straight kick; also it is a back foot kick. Better used to strike the lower parts (targets) of the body like the stomach, ribs, groin and maybe the solar plexus. Trying to strike the head with a front kick is a low percentage hit and with a slight miss or a parry from opponent you'll be easerly knocked of balance this will leave you vulnerable for a counter. Kicking to the head with a front kick can be used for an advanced fighter, not a beginner.

Application: Starting from the ready fighting position with the back foot bring it forward while lifting your knee up and thrust your foot forward towards your target. Pull your toes back and make contact with the ball of the foot.

There are three types of front kicks.

1) Thrust snap kick.- Thrust the foot forward and hit your target with a snap at the end. Bring your foot back behind you. Again remember to bring that foot back fast! Same with the push kick.

2) Committed kick.- With a committed front kick you thrust your foot forward trying to kick through your target then drop the foot down in front.

3) Push kick.- A push kick is used when your opponent comes into distance quickly, maybe to get to punching distance. If he does try you throw a front push kick to stop and push him back.

Good timing is needed for the push kick.

STRAIGHT INSIDE OUT KICK: This is a back foot kick. I use this kick because it feels natural to me. It's a kick that starts from the natural fighting position. It's a very simple kick to execute if you have some flexibility. Starting from ready fighting position (stance) just bring your back foot forward bringing your knee up and with momentum push the lower leg (below the knee) out on an angle towards your target, swivelling at the knee. The instep is the striking point so bring those toes back. This kick is great in practicing in combinations with other kicks.

Imagine you have multiple attackers.

The target areas are the – groin - Stomach

- Ribs  - Solar Plexus
- Neck - Face


BACK KICK: A back kick is used if an attacker approaches from behind but also a back kick can be performed when kicking an opponent in front of you!  In performing a back kick it needs a good sense of timing also knowing good distance that is between you and your opponent. Now this kick takes a lot of practice to get power but the main difficulty in this kick is to keep your balance.

Beginners will tend to fall forward or backwards so try and keep your weight centred through-out the kick. Make contact with the bottom (flat) part of your foot. This kick really needs a lot of patience and concentration while practicing to get the balance right. Beginners should target the lower parts of the body. The target areas are the – Knees - Groin - Stomach - Ribs

But after you get the right body action, target the throat also!

APPLICATION: Back kick to behind- From the fighting ready position look behind you keep your eyes on the attacker. Next, with the front foot lift your knee up high then kick backwards in the one motion straight towards your target behind you.

Your body will turn and after your kick drop your foot. Remember again always have your hands in a position to defend, not above your head or out to the sides.

APPLICATION: Back kick to the front- This one is a little more difficult but there is only one change. Just by using the

*(7) Pivot and hit @ 180 degrees* in the foot work section you will be facing the other way. From here you just perform the kick like kicking someone behind you! After pivoting on your heals and turning your body, lift

your knee up high and kick backwards in the one motion straight towards your target.

(Study the* pivot and hit to 180 degrees, Number (7)* in the foot work section)

# KICKING: ROUND KICKS

ROUND HOUSE KICK- (Mawashi). You can use your front foot or back foot with the round house kick. This kick is an explosive and natural kick that kicking to the head with practice will become very easy to do.

Areas to strike with the round house kick are:

- Thighs  - Stomach

- Groin    - Solar plexus

- Ribs     - Neck

- Temple - Face


BACK FOOT-

APPLICATION: Starting from fighting ready position. (Stance)

First with the round house kick move your back foot forward.  As your leg is moving forward your knee must come up. At the top of the movement roll your hip, kick in an arc towards the target. Try not to kick in too big an arc. Keep it tight and kick directly towards your target.

The movement should be an easy flowing action. Your round house kick can be a snap kick or you can kick through your target knocking your opponent or attacker out! With the round house kick you must bring your toes back and connect with the instep of the foot. Top of the foot. In a tournament as a beginner I broke my big toe kicking my opponent, connecting him on the forehead. So bring those toes back!!

Again with the round house kick practice kicking with the front and back leg. They both have good points. The back foot is an explosive powerful kick. Again don't kick in to big an arc. Be direct and put all of your weight into it while making sure to keep a nice easy body action. I prefer to use the front foot round house kick. Mainly because the front foot is closer to the target, also half the body movement is already done. There is no bringing the leg forward, it's already there to strike. Also there's less chance the opponent or attacker can telegraph it so less time he has to evade it. More chance of knocking him out!

FRONT FOOT-

APPLICATION: Starting from fighting ready position. (Stance)

You use the footwork in the foot work section. Either:

1) Forward attack

2) Forward step and slide

3) Back foot slide to strike

Choose one and from there simply kick in a tight arc straight towards the target by lifting your knee and rolling your hip simultaneously. Snapping your foot on impact. Again* Study the footwork in the foot work section.*


OUTER CRESCENT KICK- This is an explosive whipping back foot kick in which you whip your foot in an arc away from  the body striking your opponent on the side off the face or  head.

APPLICATION: Starting from fighting ready position. Just  say right foot forward. Keeping your back leg (left) straight through-out the movement bring it forward, up and across your body going away (Right to left) striking your opponent or attacker with the knife edge part of the foot. (Part that goes from the heal to the little toe.) Practice this kick to make it a beautiful fast flowing movement.

KNEES: (STRIKING)

A knee to strike is used in close quarter combat and is a powerful strike. It's easy to learn and doesn't matter if your male or female or your age. If you get a knee in you will drop anyone!

Most people have a basic under standing of kneeing, it is simple and a natural survival movement. Having a partner to practice with is best and most effective way but if practicing alone using a kick bag is sufficient. The main areas which are targeted are:

- Thighs   - Groin

- Stomach - Solar plexus

- Ribs - Face


The following are basic knee technique:

1. (A) A knee to the groin is basically only a lift of the knee. It must be accurate though or you may end up making your attacker mad! So it is mainly only the accuracy that is required.


This movement is a finishing blow if accurate.

1.   (B) If you find yourself slightly of centre (sideish) of your attacker a knee to the thigh (a corky) is effective but

this movement needs a follow up. Most likely a punch to the nose, Jaw or maybe an open hand chop strike to the throat. Whatever!

To escape the attacker!

(2) A knee to the face is a little more difficult. It is mostly used as a second movement when the attacker is dazed or leaning    over from a hit to his stomach or solar plexus, but not always however.    The face is a long distance away from your knee so to break the distance you need leverage as in grabbing his ears or hair    and pulling his head down. Also just as effective is grabbing the back of his head and pulling it down. A knee to the face is a devastating finishing blow!

Writing this however makes me want another hair cut?


So in summary:

Anyone can knee strike.

It is simple, effective strike to use if you find yourself in trouble while in close quarters.

# Strategy

In fighting you must have a plan of attack. Don't just go and start punching and kicking all over the place. Their must be a strategy. Strategy is the art of planning and directing movements of skill to win a fight.

At the beginning of a fight for an example just watch your opponent and just react to what he does. Be patient. Learn. Move, be just out of distance then bang, be on the offensive which will keep him on the defensive.

The basics in good timing and speed plus good distance and great foot work will make it easier to make a strategy work for you to knock him out!!

But again don't just parry 'n' punch, bounce around on your feet waiting for your opponent to make a mistake. You must create the winning edge!! Have a strategy, a tactic. A procedure calculated to gain some end to win the fight.

Here are some strategies:

Feints, leaving openings to counter attacks or just observing your attackers or opponents movements. Or another is a movement in the midst of a movement! A time strike is a strike done while an attacker or opponent is in the middle of their attack. To time strike you must move out of his line of attack beating him to the punch or kick by initiating his movement by great timing. So a TIME STRIKE is while the attacker or opponent is-

1) Between combinations.

2) While feinting. - If attacker feints too many times.

3) While opponent steps forward to kick or punch.

4) While your opponent is at the end of his action, when he drops his foot down after a kick or when he brings his hand back after a punch.

If a fighter bounces around or moves in rhythm, his measured flow of movements is in pattern with regulated successions of strong and weak elements in which you must watch till you find the correct time to attack. It's easy to counter attack them knowing what your attackers about to do. In fighting use variety in your movements ( techniques) and rhythm. This tactic is used while in defence and offence. A time strike obviously takes great timing, footwork but it also takes awareness. Skill in mental alertness. In practice movements need mental Visionilization, precision in timing. Be calm, relax. In time you will have awareness to move without thinking.

# OPENINGS:

First you must be aware of your opponents or attackers

movements. Like his eyes, a roll of the shoulder or movements of the arm or feet.

1) Leaving an opening for your opponent to strike you. Knowing he will strike there and when he does, counter attack, parry him and strike where he leaves an opening.

2) Observing his preparation of an attack you can adjust yourself to keep out of his line of attack and striking him where the opening occurs.


# FEINTS:

Feinting is a false move in which you are feinting an attack. Say punching, but with no intention off hitting your opponent but rather drawing him into executing a parry or block.

-It will leave you an opening in which to strike. Another words disguising a strike in one line, hopefully so he commits to parrying but attacking him on another line to your target.

- A feint is done so you can trick your opponent so you can get yourself in distance to strike him. A good fighter though Doesn't react to feints, he will keep himself just out of distance, take that half step back and move in when he is ready!

So a feint or your false move must appear to be a real attack, making your opponent to parry. Making him move on the defence.

Feints go from- High to low

- Low to high

- Left to right

- Right to left

High to high, etc many possibilities, you work it out?

To keep good distance, having good timing is great basics for fighting which is being aware of your attackers or opponents

limbs, their striking weapons.

- If he keeps his hands low, try a straight hit to his nose. If you succeed hit him with the 1,2,3,-10.Knock him down!!

If you fail in striking him high be aware and watch observe their reaction. This is where a feint comes in. Go high again if his hand went high the first time but this time with a half lunge kicking the shin, knee, groin or as high as the stomach if you dare!

Ok another easy one. This feint goes from low to high.

Practice kicking your opponent or partner in the legs or ribs with a round house ( mawashi) kick.

Now kick again at the same spot on his body with the same round house kick. On the third kick hopefully you have convinced him in being committed to blocking or parrying low but this time bring your kick over his shoulder kicking him in the head.

You can also make an effective feint going from left to right, right to left by feinting a jab or straight hit to the face but you take a small slide or half step to your right or left and striking out a wide rear hook to the jaw. It will be out of his vision.

-This one is just a simple slowish left cross made to make a reaction, quickly followed by a devastating quick right cross. There is no need to wait for a reaction on the left cross. You can stay in front of his movement. This is an example of a left to right feint.

A good feint can be one or two high strikes, doesn't matter what type of punch followed by a kick to the groin or knee.

An easy feint going from high to low. Feinting is only limited by your imagination. Think of some of your own and practice them over and over again with a partner so when you need to use them in defending yourself you will pull them off!

# THE END.

Fighting is to defend yourself only,

Fighting for the sake of fighting
is not the answer!

Love your fellow man.

All life is precious

All life has beauty

Life itself is a gift.

There are only rules & limitations man has put
upon himself. Live outside the box. If there is a
god, he is in you, not in the sky.

eg: You are your own creation!

*by Terry Birch*

# ACKNOWLEDGEMENT

I would like to acknowledge my beautiful daughter Tiarna Brooke Quadrio for her help with the pictures, some wonderful stretching poses but most of all for her computer skills, time and patience. Without Tiarna this book would not have been possible.